A Siege of Herons

To Tucker & Libby,
Thank you
for your [illegible]
and beautiful
presence here in

A Siege of Herons

The Island Keeper's Farewell

Pittsburgh.
Loving blessings,
Rebecca

Poems by
Rebecca Cole-Turner, CJN

Sycamore Island Press

ISBN 978-0-9980686-3-3

Sycamore Island Press
Gibsonville NC

Contents

FOREWORD

My poems are prayers,
close observations,
intentional thoughts
for good in the world,
arcs of pure love
flung out into the universe,
messages of hope
delivered into the ether,
celebrating Light, Love and Spirit
in service of peace.

I've been writing poetry from at least the age of ten. My mother helped me type a poem I wrote in 1960 titled "The Butterfly," my observations of a Monarch flying in the hot northern California summer sun where we lived. I thank Mom for her encouragement of and enthusiasm for my writing.

Thanks also to my Great-Uncle Laurence Calvin Smith who shared his poems with me. Also, gratitude to my fourth grade teacher, Judith Bollinger, who was kind and encouraged my writing, to my fifth grade teacher, Fred Hand, who read the *Oz* books to our class every afternoon of that year, and to my high school newspaper adviser of *The Forge,* Dorothy Westfall Brubeck, now all of Blessed Memory. My deepest thanks to my husband, Ron, who has written many lovely poems for me over the last 49 years and who has always been so encouraging of my writing. He served as my fine publishing production manager for this volume.

For the past eleven years, Jan Beatty and my friends, the Madwomen in the Attic at Carlow University, have taught me much about the art and craft of writing poetry. My dear friends in the Informal Friday Morning Madwomen group have been my constant helpful critics and encouragers. Thank you to Wendy Scott Paff who served as my Madwomen poetry mentor this spring. My whole-hearted gratitude to Jamie Benjamin, who served as my able editor *extraordinaire*, whose honesty helped me so much in preparing this manuscript. I thank all of these gifted, encouraging poets who have helped me hone my words. Any mistakes found in this book are entirely mine.

Finally, much gratitude and love to my family – Ron, Rachel, Sarah, Hal, Ben and Caroline – who've brightly born the stress of living with someone who is trying to write poetry. One of our fondest family stories goes back to a summer week we spent together at our beloved United Church of Christ Conference Center in Craigsville, MA, where I was attending the Cape Cod Writers' Conference. A Russian writer friend who lived in the other side of our cottage remarked to them one morning, *Is difficult being family of poet!* He was right. And so, with great love, this volume is dedicated to them.

With my deepest gratitude,
Rebecca Cole-Turner, CJN
October 2017

On the banks of the Allegheny River
across from Sycamore Island
Pittsburgh, PA

INTRODUCTION

I am the Island Keeper

of an oasis on the Allegheny River,
fourteen acres of undeveloped forest,
an alluvial floodplain of hardwood trees,
one of the rarest kinds of plant communities
on earth.

I've marked the past fifteen years by the flow
of the river past Sycamore Island.
Now as I end my time as the Island Keeper,
I know this island has been my Keeper as well.

AUTUMN

Sycamore Island Coordinates:
40°29'30"N 79°51'23"W / 40.49167°N 79.85639°W / 40.49167; -79.85639.

https://en.wikipedia.org/wiki/Sycamore_Island_(Pennsylvania)

Since 1809, Sycamore Island has more than doubled, from 6 to 14 acres. In 1936, the Audubon Society rented Sycamore and its smaller companion island, Nine Mile, from the Pennsylvania Railroad, creating the first bird sanctuary in Pittsburgh.

http://alleghenylandtrust.org/green-space/sycamore-island/

AUTUMN'S UNFOLDING

An estuary was created
on the river's shallow edge
from the water's slow undulation
against the shore. Gentle waves
wash up against sand, rocks,
molding detritus - fallen leaves,
snail shells, the wings of a butterfly -
into a crescent shaped like
last night's thumbnail moon.

Autumnal equinox comes
to the Allegheny. The Great Blue
flies overhead to her warm nest.
Tall trees out on Sycamore Island
begin their fall transformation –
red-orange, burnt sienna,
mahogany, maize, raw umber.

Paper-thin leaves
await winter's winds
to shake them down.

SKY OVER PEDERNAL

> *God told me that if I painted it enough,*
> *He would give it to me.*
> —Georgia O'Keeffe

I climb to Chimney Rock butte
to celebrate your coming into yourself
as well as your art now a century past.
From an eagle's eye view I see your red adobe
down below. This high desert country became
both refuge and muse: your daily walks through
these canyons and arroyos restored you.
Painting them saved you.

No man can ever do that for a woman.
You learned that lesson through
your ninety-nine years and many loves.
Tonight by the fire at Casa del Sol, moon and stars
hanging low in cobalt sky over Pedernal, I think,
God gave you this mountain after all.

TURTLE SPOTTING

The shallows along the river's edge
are transparent in early sunlight,
like the translucent blue-green
of warm seas off Belize.

I hope to see turtles but none appear.
Even the fish are hiding after the rain.
On Sycamore Island's point,
a Great Blue wades, spies fish
a diving kingfisher tries to catch.

Shadows of autumn's slow debut
appear on the water, add crimson,
flaming orange, gold to the glassy green.
Leftover crickets from hot summer days
still chirp in constant but less cacophonous chorus.

I hear faint conversation from two kayaks
approaching from downriver.
They remind me of other quiet mornings
when I, too, paddled on the Allegheny.
For today, my musings are enough for me.
I'm content to sip my Earl Grey
while keeping a watch out for turtles.

Harvest moon

rises slowly
to greet nightfall.

On pale blue sky
she paints a fire globe
with the golden glow
of a million fireflies.

On dark water, she dances
a moonbeam dance
on the Allegheny River,
my sister, Harvest Moon.

DELUGE

Swollen by hurricane rains,
dirty brown from oozing mud
dredged up from the depths below,
what looks like the Loch Ness Monster
floats past and keeps moving down river.

The birds seem to be hiding out from the recent deluge—
the turkey vultures wait in their trees for the waters
to go down so they can feast on carrion that remains.
There's no place for the Great Blue with the silver back
to fish. The water is moving too fast for the ducks.
The Canada geese have taken shelter from this storm.

Soon it will be dark and no sounds will be heard
except for the rushing of the water
and perhaps a call from the loon on her nest
as if to ask, *What now?*
And, *When?*

I dream of my island,

how it looked in 1750,
shrouded by silver mist
as the young Guyasuta,

in soft leather moccasins,
raises his bow
when the stag appears.

The fog lifts,
the pale sun
reveals the shoreline.

Guyasuta watches clouds
reflected in the blue river
before he releases his arrow.

UNFURLED

A Great Blue Heron lands at rivers edge this morning.
Perhaps summer-in-autumn weather makes her bold
and the promise of a bath is irresistible.
She unfurls her wings like the seraphim,
then dips her slender neck,
splashing as she draws it back toward her body.
Some distance away,
a fish hawk plunges into the water,
flying off with its catch.

WHAT IF THIS PLACE LOOKED AT ME?

Through a light rain
that hovers over the river,
she seems to look back at me.

She sees me through my picture windows
up here on my second floor above the river,
a sixty-six-year-old woman,
eyes cast downward at the keyboard,
attempting to write a poem about her.

I wish I could ask her how she sees me.
Questions like, *What is your view of the life
I carry on here across from you?*
And, *Do you feel too exposed by my gaze?*

I wish we could begin a kind of conversation
that would carry us into an intimacy
not often enjoyed by islands
and women who love them.

A WAND IN MY HAND

Soon the eve of All Hallows will come,
beasts of all sorts will be on the run,
black cats will creep and sit on the fence,
witches on broomsticks will make people wince.

Fairies will frolic, make mayhem grand,
while spiders and crawlies of all kinds will land
on my head, in my shoes, in so many places,
I'll be too afraid to tie my shoelaces!

Superheroes will soar, princesses will reign,
ghosties and ghoulies will fly once again.
Zombies will crash, as the Undead do—
my street will be filled with a frightful crew!

I wait for werewolves who howl, monsters who mash,
knowing leftover candy goes into MY stash!
But as always, I'm ready, my wand in my hand,
I'm the kind, white-haired grandma in tiara headband.

ALL SAINTS' DAY:
NOVEMBER 1, 2009

On this somber, hallowed evening
dusk lays down
over far hills, nearby islands,
lush with sycamore, silver maple,
lowers to shore's edge,
slips into the river.

The painter's brush at day's end
washes over land, river.
Gold, bronze, green,
muted palette of end-of-autumn,
sets the scene for mystery and holiness.

We've kept silent watch, the river and I,
for signs of saints, old and new.
On this day, I remember those loved, lost,
still so close, barely out of sight.

Horizon appears,
in what seems to be a finite boundary,
as deep-down darkness descends.
My eyesight dims
but I see now in the room beyond
all the blessed saints.

THE DAY AFTER THE ELECTION: NOVEMBER 9, 2016

Hush,
still your heart,
let the old year begin to fade.
As you bid it *adieu*,
wave goodbye,
give it your condolences,
package up its grief,
bind up the pain it brought
that still touches you
in the most tender places,
makes you wince
when you remember
November's ugly surprise.

Hush,
still your mind,
we're about to venture out onto new ice.
Be mindful of cracks
imbedded in its surface.
Admit you're frightened of possibilities
yet undiscovered, unknown.
Yes, you wish, hope, pray
there is some way to revive
your flagging spirit.
You realize all you can do is try to breathe.

Hush,
still your spirit,
open your eyes, look far beyond
your little pond, see the others
around you who, like you,
have their arms extended,
wishing, hoping, praying
for a way to move past
this unwelcomed future.
Then take someone's hand,
inhale a deep breath together,
invite Wisdom in,
remember the Alpha/Omega,
get on with the glorious work
of trying to make all things new.

LATE AUTUMN ON THE ALLEGHENY

It is so quiet out on the river now—
the jarring noises of summertime
boats and people falling into silence.
All but the last crinkled, yellowed leaves
have drifted down from the island's trees,
and only a few hardy ducks remain.
Even the Great Blues are lying low,
waiting, watching, eager to sleep away
the winter under marbled-gray skies.

Waves lap upon the russet shoreline
as a gentle breeze ruffles the water.
This is the stark season when Nature
goes underground.

WINTER

In the late 1960s, the Harbor Island Boat Club built a swimming pool, dock, barge, and offshore wooden pilings in the channel. People moored their boats to dance as hanging lights twinkled above and the bands played on. A local policeman told me that when he was a kid, the best place around to catch big bass was in our channel.

http://alleghenylandtrust.org/green-space/sycamore-island/

THIN ICE

This is the velvet moment
when deep darkness lifts
across the river
along the ridge of the hills beyond.

Perched on the eastern tip
of Sycamore Island
hugging the shoreline,
a flush of mallards
breaks out of the tight huddle
that has kept them warm and alive
overnight in sub-freezing temperatures.

They're ice skating. One-by-one,
like school children in single file formation,
each duck slowly waddles out on the fragile ice
that has formed around water's edge.

Overhead, a cloud floats by, palest gray
flows into ripe peach. One duck slips through the ice,
as if she forgot to look where she was going.

Nearby Canada geese awake, leisurely float
around as if to greet them, and perhaps suggest
that new ice is thinnest and not to be trusted.

Old man-in-the-moon hangs low

over icy river.
In thin blue light
of early dawn,
he smiles, winks
as if to say,
You'll be just fine.

I follow the rhythms of Nature,
of the flow of life,
not gathering too much detritus.

My good friend reminds me,
We're not nouns. We're verbs.
Growing, becoming.

Sheets of river ice
veil the water below.
Nothing moves.
But in the dark muck
at the bottom of the river,
tiny cells,
minute marine life,
live
and move
and have their being.

BUFFLEHEAD DUCKS: *Bucephala albeola*

On the grayest of gray mornings,
I awake too early, creep down the stairs
and wait in the shadows
for what day's first light will reveal.

Five tiny ducks dip their black-and-white heads
up and down then plunge beneath the river ice.
They stay down so long I think they're dead.
I wait for them to reappear, hold my breath,
slowly count – *one, two, three, four, five* –
release the air from my lungs with a loud gasp.

Just when I think all is lost,
up pops one, then another and another,
like bobbleheads you get at a Pirate's game,
or fans bobbing up and down after a homerun.

RIVER MOONSCAPE

Half-moon hangs over
the frozen landscape.
Diamonds of river ice
make the rising steam
look like ghosts
creeping low
across the water.
On hilltop ridge beyond,
naked trees stand
against a pink sky.
Up above,
in a deepening blue,
Sister Moon slowly rises
to greet the Evening Star.

EARLY MORNING

Sun breaks through to warm the river.
Most of the Canada geese have flown further South.
Only a quartet remains.
With their black-webbed feet, they walk gingerly
on thin sheets of cracking ice.

I imagine their conversation goes something like this:
Well, do you think we should take off?
    No, I'd like to eat some more grubs before the flight.
But if we don't go now, we'll fall in, get our feathers
    wet, and have to take off from the frigid water!
    Oh, all right!
Okay, Grumpy, let's get going then! You first.

FULL COLD MOON:
CHRISTMAS MORNING 2015

6 a.m., cup of hot coffee in hand,
I watch the Allegheny,
muddied by recent rain,
as logs, human debris
lazily float down river.

My old friend the beaver
searches for logs to secure his dam.
He swims to each willow, pauses,
looks up at tender shoots, rejects them,
moves on.

A Full Cold Moon illuminates the beaver's task.
He stands tall, stretches as far as his paws can reach,
uses his long flat tail for balance.
This is the tree he's been searching for.
He attacks the branches,
chomps them off with his orange buck teeth.
Then with a loud *SMACK!* of his tail,
he swims downstream with his bounty.

JANUARY 1, 2008, ON THE ALLEGHENY

A million or more diamonds
jeté across the surface
of river glass.
Joy fills my aging heart.
In the sun dance,
Sycamore Island rests
in bright light.
A silver maple
in the foreground
stands at water's edge,
a talisman for the new year.

A TRINITY OF HERONS:
NEW YEAR'S DAY 2014

A trinity of Great Blue Herons
graces my river this morning.

The one I call *Silverback*
strafes the cold green water
almost wetting his wings.
His smaller mate, cobalt blue,
follows him down river, higher,
faster than his slow, steady rhythm.

Later, an even smaller heron
flies in the same direction,
lands in the white-barked sycamore.

TOO EARLY

I wake up in the middle of a night
that's darker than India ink.
Geese squawk as if there's a fox
roaming the island.

I take my tea to the window.
The Canada geese paddle to my side
of the river, forage below.

One gander unfurls his wings,
lowers his head, hurls himself
toward another gander.

Could they be starting to mate
in late January?

If so, they're in for heartbreak.
Last spring, the high water
kept rising, drowning their eggs.

I tell them, *Slow down,*
ease up, play hard to get,
let the girls pursue you.
Don't be in such a rush.
Let the water recede first.

SILVER-BACK HERON

The snow falls deep.
All is still on this frozen
ribbon of river.
He comes,
quietly flies low,
strafes the water surface,
first one wing, then the other.
Silver-backed, wise.
Gracefully, he shows up,
eases the pain,
reminds me of the Holy.

EARLY BLOOMS

My paperwhites
bloomed early this year,
overnight while I was sleeping.

The box of crusty brown bulbs
claimed it would take six weeks
after my New Year's Day planting

for the four of them
to shoot up, burst
into delicate white flowers.

But here they are
this morning, peeping out
from their green sheaths,

enticing me to put my nose close,
breathe in their heady, delicious scent,
and dream of a warm spring.

HIBERNATION

In the corner by my study window,
blooming paperwhites fill the air
with their sweet-honey fragrance,
a welcome taste of spring
coming in the middle of winter's deep freeze.
I count on four dry bulbs carefully planted
on New Year's Day to carry me
through the white/gray chill of long January days,
though I know they never bloom
until near its frozen ending.
But strong days of sun early on have forced
an earlier flowering, and I am glad of it—
two weeks of sub-freezing temperatures
have left my spirits sagging, my body hurting.
Every step I take on snow with black ice underneath
leaves me hoping I won't fall.

This morning a gaggle of a hundred geese
are hunkered down wing-tip-to-wing-tip
out on the ice bridge that has formed
from shore to Sycamore Island.
Like Russian soldiers clustered together
in drab brown uniforms
trying to survive Siberia's frigid wasteland,
they are so still, so quiet, in stark contrast

to the chaotic cacophony of loud squawking
and honking that will resume in early spring
when the uproar of mating season begins.

Tiny black-and-white Bufflehead Ducks
keep their feathered Canada friends company
as they float around the goose-filled ice flow,
diving in and out of the river for fun and breakfast.
A Red-tailed Hawk flies from a distant treetop—
I wonder if she has made the island her home?

Meanwhile, my Great Blues are nowhere to be seen.
I miss them, my companions in the snowy gloom.
But thoughts of turtles deep down in warm mud
brings cheer and a smile to my face,
and I know that my hibernation
will also end in due season.

PAPERWHITES

They are blooming in the corner
by my window, exotic fragrance
strong in the undiluted sunlight.
I want to bathe in their perfume,
and float in their fragile beauty.
Early harbingers of spring, though
I have brutally forced their flowering
from ugly dormant brown bulbs.
They give me some hope that winter
won't last forever and that I, too,
will find a way to bloom again.

Soon it will be time

for the fox
to trot out
to Sycamore Island.
First, one paw
on the thin ice
near shore
to test for thickness.
Carefully,
nose in the air
to smell danger,
then one paw
in front of another,
he reaches the shoreline
of his sanctuary.

No danger there,
no predators.
Soft snow falls,
covering his red fur.

THE DAY THE FLOODING STARTED

Overnight the Allegheny River rose several feet.
Swollen by ice plates, it moves silently,
changes Sycamore Island's landscape.

Huge chunks of ice flow swiftly downriver,
sweep up everything in their path,
bring with them big barrels of refuse.

No Canada geese this morning,
nor mallards waiting for the thaw.
As it rushes to meet the Ohio River,
its churning waters make a clean sweep
of the land as we know it.

SPRING

One afternoon in 2005, I was alarmed when I saw smoke rising from the center of Sycamore Island. With my trusty binoculars, I saw three men around a large, roaring campfire so I called the Blawnox Fire Department. Fifteen minutes later, a motor boat sped toward the island. Arms in the air, the interlopers were escorted off the island after the fire was doused.

ALLEGHENY SPRING

A gentle wind breathes
over the river, rippling
its emerald green face.

These are the first signs
of spring on the Allegheny.
Green buds on trees,
ducks and geese coupled,
flapping noisily, eager to mate,
cotton-tufted pussy willows
along water's edge,
a robin with straw in its beak,
yellow daffodils peeping up
through rough brown soil,
signs of beaver chomping
on weeping willow trees.

I have a deep yearning to take off
my winter coat and boots
and wade in smooth silky brown silt.

MATING FOR LIFE

High above the greening river,
two red-tailed hawks glide,
soar upward
in whirling concentric ballet.

A wing dips here,
another wing lifts there,
until they light side-by-side.

What do they know
about their fitness as mates?
Not their partner's DNA,
how it will blend with their own.

Mating for life
can be a scary proposition.

RIVER PRAYER

The moon wanes,
the mad chaos
of its fullness erased.

Too much water flows downstream
to God-knows-where,
homes, farmland lost in its wake,
boats, people swept away.

You can have too much of a good thing.
I wish Nature would slow down,
turn off her faucet, let the ducks
lay eggs, welcome kayaks,
canoes once again.

VERNAL EQUINOX

Yesterday's mad flow of ice
coloring the river white
has vanished.

The hawk takes off
from her sycamore tree perch
in search of food to break fast.

Muddy landscape awaits
nesting of ducks and geese,
turtles not far behind.

I pray for ducks

and geese, too,
especially when they nest.
I meditate daily on the innate
goodness of Great Blue Herons.

After a too-warm winter
it's been a too-cold spring,
yet the birds still sit
in their nests on time.

I thought all was well.
But this morning I saw the roots
of the willows along the edge
of the Allegheny covered in cold water.

Which means the ducks and geese
that didn't make their nests
on higher ground found their eggs
flooded and will now abandon them.

RIVER DANCE

Awake before first birdsong,
I creep downstairs to make hot chocolate.
Turning to view the river with cup in hand,
I see gray ghosts dance silently around
the island perimeter, rise up to shroud
trees and hillside. Sweeping, soaring,
gliding upon the river, silver phantoms
whisper a primordial song.

TWO SYCAMORE TREES

Before the sun is up
over the far distant hill,
before the nesting geese
move off their warm eggs,
before the Great Blue Heron,
the one with silver-tipped wings,
makes her inaugural morning flight
to scout out deep pools where
the fish are gathering in the first rays
of sunlight, two sycamore trees
stand tall across the river
on the greened island.
They are of equal height,
smaller than the oak trees, set apart
from each other by thick Japanese knotweed,
as straight as telephone poles dotting
landscape beyond. One is in the sunlight:
the other remains in the shadows.
Spindly, uneven branches, sparse foliage
covers the darker one, while its almost-twin
carries its verdant, lush greenery spread evenly
in all directions from its center core.
I marvel at the difference that sunshine makes
on two identical seeds, rooted
in the same rich soil, on the same river bank,
on the same day, on island primeval.

THE ART OF HOLY/WHOLLY LISTENING

The listening, then,
becomes a bridge.
Such close, loving attentiveness
to shadows, light,
the in-between spaces
and nuanced meanings
hidden beneath words,
turned over midstream
like weighty river rocks
obstructing the flow,
allows new vision,
fresh perspective,
a more transparent noticing
of Spirit's wisdom.
Perhaps a passageway
blocked by the rough rubble
of an aching heart
is cleared away,
dense detritus removed,
reconnecting us to the Source.
Together with the Holy,
we cross a stream called Mystery,
emerging on the other side,
revived, restored,
and newly awake
in the Presence.

HERON PILGRIMAGE

On Sycamore Island's shrouded tip,
the Great Blue stands silent watch
over river, sand, trees and sky,
an early morning avian sentinel,
guardian of this green water passage.

The heron dips his beak
into shallow water seeking fish.
Monastic in his stillness,
he makes no waves, not even a ripple.

Like a priest at prayer, he glides down river.
The gray monk extends his feathered head.
With halting gait his slender body follows,
like an old Benedictine brother
taking his early morning constitutional.

Do herons pray?
And, if so, for what?

ETERNAL STORY

Darkened dusk
on still waters,
minimal light,
limited sight.

Cloud cover
pink and gray,
shadows grow,
boaters row.

Monarchs migrate,
snails meander,
Kingfishers dive,
turtles thrive.

Creator's icons
by river's edge,
tree and flower,
bird in bower.

SUMMER

One morning in 2007, I saw a hand-painted sign on the island's tip that read: "Island for sale - $250,000" with a phone number to call. I panicked, called my friend Jane Ockershausen, who also helps protect Sycamore as my fellow Island Keeper, and said, "We've got to find a way to buy the island!" Fortunately, the Allegheny Land Trust bought it on January 28, 2008, and funds for its conservation were given by the Colcom Foundation. Jane and I were part of the first group that helped envision a plan to preserve and take care of it for future generations.

The wild things

take flight
as silver river mists rise.
On emerald island's edge,
a solitary Great Blue remains.
She lifts her feathered head,
then takes slow, measured
steps into deeper water.
Ever so slowly, the heron
stretches slender neck high
until it finally reaches zenith:
her body abruptly freezes
like a soldier on watch stills
when a distant target is sighted.
Suddenly, silvered fish is snatched
and slithers down the narrow throat.
Savoring the meal, she pauses,
then great wings unfurl and lift
heavy body on thin legs into air.

DANCE OF THE TURKEY VULTURE

I see a silver fish
dead on shore,
scales glistening
water washing
over the carcass.

Who'll discover it?
Who'll eat it first?

A turkey vulture,
resident of *Turkey Vulture Beach*
on the other side of the island,
lands, plucks out the eyes,
devours the brain,
hops up on the fish,
does a turkey vulture happy dance.

A flotilla of Canada geese arrives.
The vulture flies off
but soon brings back another.

The armada of geese circles
the carcass. Vultures approach,
peck at it again.
Geese swim away.

MIDSUMMER MUD

Before heat of the day rises up,
the surprising coolness
of morning greets the mallards

who glide on the river
like silent ice skaters. Down below,
a hare hops through purple loosestrife,

pausing to munch on grass.
I saw a fawn yesterday on Sycamore Island
after spotting hoof prints in shoreline mud.

The box turtles begin to stir in the water
as the Red-winged Blackbird sings
to the still sleeping earth.

ON THE DIRT ROADS OF OUR CHILDHOOD:
REDWOOD VALLEY, CALIFORNIA, 1956-1962

My best friend Vicky and I
could easily catch them
when they ventured out
from underneath lacy ferns
after a long soaking rain.
Back then, salamanders roamed
our forest floor in abundance.

Six years we played together
with these amphibians.
They're about 6 inches long,
slippery, shiny orange skin
with brown backs,
big yellow eyes that protrude,
tiny nostrils and mouths
that look like they're smiling.

They sashay on four crooked legs,
close to the ground,
use their long tails,
four-fingered hands,
and five-fingered feet
to propel themselves.

Vicky called them *waterdogs*.
We picked them up never knowing
their skin exudes a toxin
that can kill you if eaten
or rubbed into broken skin.

When I call her each year
on her Epiphany birthday,
I always ask how many waterdogs
she's seen up on our hill.
This year, she saw only one.

TREE TRUNK BUDDHA, AYUTTHAYA, THAILAND: JULY 2002

There are still one thousand Buddhas,
some golden and reclining
within the ancient island city of Ayutthaya,
most of their heads decapitated
by Burmese marauders
two hundred fifty years ago.
I found a face of the Buddha
that is now trapped,
lifted up from the dusty ground
where it fell,
surrounded and held up
by the thick roots
of a gnarled, old Bodhi tree.
Looking at his weathered form,
I asked him questions
that have me puzzled –
Can I be connected to others yet not trapped?
Can I desire yet not suffer?
Can I be enlightened yet not lose myself?
Still smiling,
the Buddha winked,
and I began to understand
as his root prison disappeared
into nothingness.

RIVER MANNERS

Like smooth green glass
the river flows undisturbed
save for the almost silent,
steady slice of two oars.
A man looks up,
sees me smile down at him,
gives a quick nod,
smiles, tips his hat
without breaking stride.

CIRCLES

As a still pond on a clear summer day,
I sit silently in the Presence,
breathing in,
breathing out,
prayer dropping like a small pebble
on waiting water surface,
creating concentric circles
rippling center to edge and back again,
this time set aside to tend the Holy,
watching each successive wave as it appears,
deeply pondering Spirit's undulations
within and without.

I LOVE OTTERS

Scientists have found a cranium
of an ancient sea otter in China's Yunnan Province.
I'm a lover of otters, both river and sea.
You could say they're my totem
so strong is their pull on me from childhood.
A perfect summer day for me back then
was a day on the Mendocino coast,
running after sea gulls and pelicans,
watching sea otters surf and play
with their babies on their bellies.
They would dive down deep
to crack oysters on rocks
on the bottom of the ocean.

These extinct otters were as big as mastiffs,
far bigger than the smaller ones I used to watch.
I could have ridden them like a dolphin.

But could I have loved the giants they were?

PRAIRIE CREEK REDWOODS:
SUMMER 1973

We hike through the Old Ones,
the tallest trees on earth,
while bees buzz a low tune in our ears.

Ferns tickle our ankles.
We breathe the loamy scent
of decayed wood on forest floor.

The insistent *tap! tap! tap!*
of an Acorn Woodpecker makes us
crane our necks to see

the roof of forest made up
of two thousand year old
shaggy Coast Redwoods.

Waves crash on shore.
As we come into a clearing,
an elk saunters by.

PILGRIMAGE/SANCTUARY

Church bells peal in the distance.
The low rumbling of a train
slowly passing by reminds me
I am home at last.

Pilgrimage is always an uprooting
from safe, familiar territory
into a new unknown.
Its reward, a quiet time
of sitting back, sinking in,
breathing air I've breathed before,
time to ponder what I have learned.

This river,
these rocks,
this island,
these trees,
give safety I can tuck back into,
finding deep comfort.
Yet without you beside me,
on pilgrimage or not,
no place is the sanctuary I seek.

AFTERWORD

QUEST

In memory of my father, Eugene Cole, Sr.
August 26, 1919 – September 9, 2011

Deep indigo of darkening twilight
illuminates his tall form
between the willow trees.

Stepping out only after
his long beak and stretched neck
lead him haltingly forward,

the Great Blue lingers as if
to savor the calm and quiet
of the night that covers him

as he makes his way along
the island's edge. Now and then,
he pauses and his beak darts

into the water shadows. Sometimes
he pulls up a wriggling, silvered fish
but other times he misses his catch.

Mostly, he seems content to spend
his time in the habitat he's been given,
a solitary heron alone on his quest.

VERLA NADINE SMITH COLE

In memory of my mother,
June 22, 1926 – October 26, 2016

I search for her all day
in my memory, old pictures,
her journals from the early forties.
She was 15 when she met my sailor father,
World War II raging.

It would have been her 91st birthday.
I want to celebrate my mother,
thank her for my life,
her whimsy, laughter,
her humor, music.

But somehow,
she eludes me,
seems to be
just around the corner,
hidden behind a veil.

Dusk falls,
quiets river music.
I walk out on my deck,
look down at the Japanese knotweed,
find her there
in the flashing of fireflies.

THE ISLAND KEEPER'S FAREWELL

Now I begin to say
my goodbyes to all my people,
my places.
I stagger them,
let them fall
as wordless blessings
on the halls
of seminary, church,
my river, my island,
poet friends,
friends who pray,
friends who dance.
I pack each box,
re-paint each wall.
I say goodbye
to the twenty-one years,
one-third of my life—
times of joy,
times of strife—
that mark my farewell passage.

ACKNOWLEDGEMENTS

The author wishes to acknowledge the following publications in which these poems first appeared, sometimes in earlier versions: *Carlow University Magazine* ("Thin Ice"); *Hungry Hearts, A Quarterly Journal of Reformed Spirituality* ("Holy/Wholly Listening"); *Pittsburgh Theological Journal* ("Circles"); *Voices from the Attic*, Carlow University Press ("Tree Trunk Buddha: Ayutthaya, Thailand: July 2002," Vol. XIII, "Sky Over Pedernal," Vol. XVI, "The wild things," Vol. XVII, "Late Autumn on the Allegheny" and "Paperwhites," Vol. XVIII, "Quest" and "Two Sycamore Trees," Vol. XIX, "Autumn's Unfolding" and "Deluge," Vol. XX, "Hibernation" and "Vernal Equinox," Vol. XXI, "Thin Ice" and "Unfurled," Vol. XXII, "The Day the Flooding Started" and "Early Blooms in Thirty Days," XXIII, forthcoming).

I am grateful to Thomas Jay Oord for permission to use his stunning photograph of a Great Blue Heron in flight on the cover of this volume. Photo ©2016 by Thomas Jay Oord. All rights reserved.

Sincerest thanks to the Allegheny Land Trust for purchasing and preserving Sycamore Island for the enjoyment of the many generations to come, the young keepers of the natural world who will explore this beautiful place and learn about Nature from it.

I want to thank Jan Beatty, Director of Creative Writing, the Madwomen in the Attic Writing Workshops, and teacher in the non-residency MFA program at Carlow University; my friends in the Informal Friday Morning Madwomen group (Jamie Benjamin, Kay Comini, Marilyn Marsh Noll, Liane Ellison Norman, Christine Pasinski, Joanne Samraney, M.A. Sinnhuber, Lucienne Wald, and Dorothy Holley and Lois Greenberg of Blessed Memory); and all the other wonderful Madwomen in the Attic, for listening to my poems and helping me learn to write better.

My deepest appreciation and admiration for the patience, creativity, and fine publishing talents of my husband, Ron Cole-Turner. Thank you, Ron, once again for your support, and thanks, too, for the support, great suggestions and love from the family we created together: Sarah, Hal, Ben and Caroline Vincent, and Rachel Cole-Turner. I couldn't have done it without all of you!

I also wish to thank the many well-loved friends and family members in my life for their love, good humor, support and encouragement. Now of Blessed Memory: my parents, Nadine and Gene Cole; Great-Grandmothers Sadie Catherine Clark Smith and Nancy Jane Lillard Atchley; Grandmother Tennessee Eva Atchley Smith Bielar and Grandfather El Bielar; Great-Uncle Larry Smith, Uncle Ben and Aunt Dolly Cole; Ann and Leonard Peck; Betty and Dick Haven; Barbara Gerber and Nancy Hale; and Clara Butow. Also, my cousins, Linda and Dale Bisby, Lisa Christensen, Don and Mary Cole; Sister-In-Love Rosemary Knerium Turner; niece and nephew Bethany and Darryl Lockie; my sisters-in-law and their husbands, Joanne and Dean Ensey and Janet and Phil Jamieson; dear friends Lisa Phelps (and her husband, Dick Alcorn, now of Blessed Memory), Erin and Dave Vickers, Kathy and Bill Liddicoet, Carol and Jay Swanson, Shantia and Jonathan Wright-Gray, Christine and Carl Shesler, Karen and Paul Lewis, Joan and Allen Hogge, Sally and Victor Vogel, Theresa Heidrich, Emily Rosenthal and John Buckley, Bernie Tickerhoof, Pan and Carl Awsumb, Kathryn Schreiber, Julia Bolton Holloway, Jane Ockershausen and Jerry Bloch, David and Marti Peck, Hester and Wentzel Van Huyssteen, Kara and Jared Georgi, Linda Baum, Jane and Robert Brawley, Jo-Ann Hoffman, Jamie Benjamin and Larry Gesoff, Jackie and James Vincent, Yung Hee and Heup Young Kim, Graham Standish, Jana and Gene Roche, Don and LindaJo McKim, Ruth and Rex Becker and all our fabulous United Church of Christ and Mystic Heart Community Chautauqua Institution friends, my oldest friend from Redwood Valley, CA, Victoria (Vicky) Buckley, my Santa Barbara High School, CA, friends Mary Zurbuchen, Devaughn Williams and Barbara Evans, my college friends R. Roland (Rip) Hodson, Jim and Diane Dixon; my *Anamchairde* Gathering soul friends (Althera Bergren, Bob Bevier, Tom Eisenmann, Jill Holseth, Susan Kemper, Cecile Lyons, Kathy McKay, Geoff Nelson, Tara Ross, Ted Scott, Sue Ann Yarbrough, and Kim Smith-Nilsson of Blessed Memory); my Peer Group Supervision and fellow spiritual director friends (Mary Lynn Callahan, Doris Dyen, Lynn Holden, Jan Klemicks, Belinda Kent, Mary Louise McCollough, Pat Mahoney, Diane Rusch, Barbara Shuman, and Betty Voight); my InterPlay Pittsburgh friends (Richard Citrin, Lynn Coghill, Sheila Collins, Amy Couch, LaVerne Darnell, Jim Holland, Lois McClendon, Pam Meadowcroft, Shari Mastalski, Gail Ransom, Neil Straub, Laurie Tarter, and Bob Wilson); my International Association of Women Ministers friends; my wonderful Women's Book Group members; my students and pilgrims in the Spiritual Formation Certificate Program at Pittsburgh Theological Seminary; my Companions of Julian of Norwich friends around the globe; and all my friends at Smithfield United Church of Christ and East Liberty Presbyterian Church, Pittsburgh.

DEDICATION OF POEMS

Autumn

"Autumn's Unfolding" is for Diane and Jim Dixon.

"Sky Over Pedernal" is for Rachel Cole-Turner.

"Turtle Spotting" is for Rosemary Knerium Turner.

"Harvest moon" is for Don and Mary Browning Cole.

"I dream of my island," is for Marti and Dave Peck.

"A Wand in my Hand" is for Caroline and Ben Vincent.

"All Saint's Day" is for Barbara Gerber and Nancy Hale.

"The Day After the Election: November 9, 2016" is for Kathy and Bill Liddicoet.

"Late Autumn on the Allegheny" is for Jung Hee and Heup Young Kim.

Winter

"Thin Ice" is for Jamie Benjamin and Larry Gesoff.

"Old Man-in-the-Moon hangs low" is for Theresa Heidrich.

"Bufflehead Ducks" is for Emily Rosenthal and John Buckley.

"Early Morning" is for Hal Vincent.

"Full Cold Moon: Christmas Morning 2015" is in memory of Dolly and Ben Cole.

"January 1, 2008, on the Allegheny" is for Sheila Collins and Rich Citrin.

"A Trinity of Herons: New Year's Day 2014" is for Carol and Jay Swanson.

"Silver-Back Heron" is for Shantia and Jonathan Wright-Gray.

"Early Blooms" is for Sarah Vincent.

"Hibernation" is for Hester and Wentzel Van Huyssteen.

"Paperwhites" is for Julia Bolton Holloway.

"Soon it will be time" is for Ben Vincent.

"The Day the Flooding Started" is for Christine and Carl Shesler.

Spring

"Allegheny Spring" is for Lisa Christensen.

"I pray for ducks" is for Don and LindaJo McKim.

"River Dance" is for Karen and Paul Lewis.

"Two Sycamore Trees" is for Kara Keding Georgi.

"The Art of Holy/Wholly Listening" is for my *Anamchairde* Gathering soul friends.

"Heron Pilgrimage" is for Lisa Phelps.

"Eternal Story" is for Bethany and Daryl Lockie.

Summer

"The wild things" is for Mary Zurbuchen, Devaughn Williams, and Barbara Evans.

"Dance of the Turkey Vulture" is for Jane Ockershausen.

"Midsummer Mud" is for Pan and Carl Awsumb.

"On the Dirt Roads of our Childhood: Redwood Valley, California, 1956-1962" is for Victoria Buckley.

"Tree Trunk Buddha, Ayutthaya, Thailand: July 2002" is for R. Roland (Rip) Hodson.

"River Manners" is for Graham Standish.

"Circles" is for my Peer Supervision Group spiritual director
    friends.

"I Love Otters" is for Caroline Vincent.

"Prairie Creek Redwoods" is for Linda and Dale Bisby.

"Pilgrimage/Sanctuary" is for Ron.

Afterword

"Quest" is in memory of my father, Eugene Cole, Sr.

"Verla Nadine Smith Cole" is in memory of my mother.